MARIE VITOCHOVÁ JINDŘICH KEJŘ JIŘÍ VŠETEČKA

PRAGUE

MOTHER
OF CITIES

V RÁJI

ISBN 80-85894-30-0

PRAGUE

capital of the Czech Republic, can rightly rank high among the most beautiful cities of Europe. For centuries has the city developed to its unique beauty being guarded from two sides by ancient castles, located on rocks above the Vltava river – the Prague Castle and Vyšehrad. Burgess houses, temples, and palaces of various architectural styles have retained spirit of the ancient times of its origin, human skills and work, sorrow and joy, and the message of its creators pass over to us as well as the next generations. Ceremonial parades held to honor the rulers and festive processions walked throughout the city. Delegations from abroad brought good as well as bad news. Merchants from distant regions and church dignitaries came, but the songs and chorals also sounded, when the crowds of Hussite people of Prague rushed through to the city walls to defend their homes. On more than one occassion has the city and both castles have been ocupied by foreign usurpers or suffered the oppression of their local allies. But every time it recovered, put things in order, and freely breathed out once more.

The golden Prague, the hundred-spired Prague, the mother of cities, the city on Vltava, as it is, beside others, called, hospitably receives numerous visitors and admirers. Whoever has got even a bit of sense of beauty and history, he will imprint its picture in his memory forever. In few places will a visitor find such a number of various building styles, memorials, or romantic corners in relatively small places. Whoever gets absorbed by the streets of Old Town, waits to see the review of apostles beneath the Old Town astrological clock, stands in a quiet meditation in front of the Bethlehem Chapel or gets carried away by the Prague Castle's panorama viewed from the embankment, and then across the Charles Bridge – an ancient artery of the city – crosses over to the picturesqueness of Lesser Town and its palace gardens, he will keep coming back to Prague.

We love our city and we want to share our impressions with you through the words and pictures, and invite you for walks around the historical and other attractive places. Let us go and see together the Prague Castle, Hradčany, Lesser Town, Old Town and New Town. Our journey ends symbolically at the ancient Vyšehrad with its spirit of old Czech legends and prophecies of the city's greatness and happy future for the entire country.

PRAGUE CASTLE

Prague Castle, the ancient residence of the Přemysl dynasty and Czech kings, has for centuries been a symbol of the Czech statehood. It forms such a panorama for the capital city that only a few cities in Europe and the world can display.

The foundation of Prague Castle goes back to 880's, when the prince Bořivoj transferred his residence here from Levý Hradec. Princely castle site was developing on an elongated ridge descending to the Vltava river and protected in a natural way on the northern side by the deep valley of Brusnice creek and there where Lesser Town extends today, by steep cliffs. In the West by a moat, carved out in rock. In its time the princely residence formed an extensive unit with buildings made from wood and stone including the church buildings. It was also protected by a mound fortification. Even a praising report of the Arab-Jewish merchant Ibrahim Ibn

A romantic view of the Prague Castle from Jan Palach Square. Rudolfinum, gorgeous Neo-Renaissance buildings by architects J. Zítek and J. Schulz. Rudolfinum represents a musical oasis of Prague. A concert music often sounds there and it became world-famed for the concerts of Prague Spring

Jákub from as long ago as 965 testifies to its imposing size.

The prince Václav (Wenceslas), patron of the Czech land, who has been sanctified for his deeds, is the most well-known princely ruler of the first half of the 10th century. The rotunda of St. Vitus was added to the oldest small church of Virgin Mary during his reign at the end of the 9th century. It was replaced by a Romanesque basilica at the end of the 11th century. In earlier times, Václav's father, Vratislav I, founded the small church of St. George by which Boleslav II established the first convent for women in Bohemia. Although, today's triple-naved basilica with two white towers represents only the result of an extensive reconstruction following the fire caused by the siege of the castle by Konrád of Znojmo in 1142.

The eastern part of the castle complex, terminated by the Black Tower, offers a less known panorama of the Prague Castle from the Intercontinental hotel. Saint Vitus Cathedral and white towers of the St. George basilica stick up above the roofs of castle palaces. Neo-baroque palace above Vltava bank is the seat of the Office of Cabinet of the Czech Republic

PRAGUE CASTLE

There are painted emblems of the clerks of Land Records in the room of New Land Records, which is accessible from the Vladislav Hall by a stairway. The walls and the emblems on them used to be sorted according to the set rules, which had to take in consideration the respective office

Not until the 1130's did the fundamental conversion of the Prague Castle into a properly fortificated castle with a princely palace and other administrative buildings take place. Soběslav I initiated this action. The Castle was gradually gaining the appearance of a stone residence – an extensive welt with towers, palace chapel of All Saints, and a masonry wall from limestone on the perimeter of the castle. The archbishop of Prague also had his residence at the Castle since the end of the 10th century. Not until the Luxemburg period, in 1344, was the bishopric promoted to archbishopric, and the Castle became the residence of the first Czech metropolitan Arnošt of Pardubice. To deserve this honor, Charles IV, with the consent of his father John Lucemburský, initiated the construction of the magnificent cathedral of St. Vitus under the guidance of French master Mathias of Arras. Reconstruction of the Royal Palace itself began already in the 1330's.

Prague Castle became the representative residence of the Holy Roman Empire's ruler and Czech king, and political, social, and construction activity did not slow down during the reign of Charles IV. The ruler's grandiose plans for a dignified residence for him and his successors were scheduled for years in advance. Unfortunately, not all was successfully completed during his reign. Activities were gradually slowing down and incompleted work was abandoned during the reign of Václav IV, who by far did not reach the qualities of his father. The importance of the castle as an executive and administrative headquarters was on the decline overall, and the fact that rulers were not residing there until the end of the 15th century confirms this statement. The Castle was first occupied by the adherents of the Roman king Zikmund during the

The Crown Chamber, which has to be open by seven locks of the seven key owners, is accessible from the Saint Wenceslas Chapel through a stairway. Coronation jewels are usually exhibited during rare occasions only. Golden Saint Wenceslas crown originated in the Charles IV'era. It was made in 1346 and enriched with gems after 1374. Sceptre and apple originated in the beginning of the 17th century – period of Rudolf II

Hussite revolution, but since the spring of 1421 it was already controlled by Hussite Prague.

Not until the Jagellon period did the Castle begin to flourish again and its construction activity became revived. A new fortification was reinforced above the Deer Moat by the characteristic columnar towers of Mihulka, White (Bílá), and Daliborka. Reconstruction of the Royal Palace took place in the spirit of Vladislav Gothic with the first elements of Renaissance. Then originated Vladislav Hall, the largest secular space of medieval Prague, according to the plans of Benedikt Ried of Pístov. The hall extends the entire third floor of the Royal Palace. There important meetings, for example assemblies or ruler's feasts during significant occasions, or even knightly tilts took place. Star-shaped vault and large windows, whose exterior sides already carry the elements of Renaissance, give a monumental impression. Also worth noticing is the main ceremonial stairway leading to Vladislav Hall (so called Rider Stairway), the Green Room, and two other Late Gothic rooms, decorated with coats of arms of the lands of the Czech Crown as well as members of the Chamber and Courtyard. An archive of Land Records used to be located here, too. Hans Spiess of Frankfurt is the author of these spaces. Still Benedikt Ried of Pístov built at this stage of the castle's conversion at the beginning of the 16th century so called Ludvík wing of palace already in a pure Renaissance style. In Czech history it is most memorable for the fact that the catholic vice-regents were thrown from the windows of the "Czech Office", located on the third floor. This occured on May 23, 1618 and initiated the Czech Uprising.

Still prior to this event the Castle had enjoyed the extraordinary favor of the Habsburgs, who ascended the Czech throne following the death of Ludvík Jagellonský near Moháč in 1526. The medieval castle was turned into a luxurious Renaissance residence during the Ferdinand I's reign. Even the famous Royal Garden with Summer Palace, where the Singing Fountain attracts the greatest attention of visitors, was founded at that time beyond the Deer Moat.

However, the true boom of activity, comparable with Charles' era, was experienced by Prague Castle during Rudolf II's reign. He resided here almost continuously. New halls (Spanish Hall and Rudolf Gallery in the northern section of buildings lining the second court) and gardens originated, the emperor became surrounded by many artists, alchemists and often questionable „creators" of the elixir of life, or gold. Basically all were welcome here, and if they satisfied the interests of emperor, they made their living – at least for the time being. Many officers of the armies of mercenaries in the following Thirty Year's War could tell stories about the quality of Rudolf's collection of arts and valuables. Following a brief period in 1619–1620, when Prague Castle was the residence of Czech king Fridrich V Falcký, the Habsburgs chose not to reside permanently in the Castle. The so called Terezian reconstruction in the se-

Saint Vitus Cathedral – a view through the main nave, which originated near the completion of the temple, all the way to the original choir with altar. The main nave connects to a medieval Parléř's choir and carries a portrait gallery of the busts of men who through their work contributed to the completion of the temple in the 19th and 20th century

Gorgeous window decoration in the Archbishop Chapel of St. Vitus Cathedral. Leaded glass in the chapel's window is a late Art Nouveau work by A. Mucha from 1931. It was donated by the former Slavia bank "to God praise, to homeland glory, to art honor", as the sign reads. Mucha's subjects were scenes from the lives of Cyril and Methode

Saint Wenceslas Chapel represents a work of Gothic at its zenith and on its construction participated Mathias of Arras and Peter Parléř. In place of the chapel used to stand since the beginning of the 10th century the rotunda of St. Vitus, whose founder was St. Václav (Wenceslas). Jindřich (Henry) Parléř created the statue of St. Václav, standing on a ledge above the altar, in 1373. A Gothic tombstone of St. Václav from the 14th century stands in the middle of the chapel. It was renewed in 1912 – 1913

PRAGUE CASTLE

cond half of the 18th century, which gave it today's appearance of extensive palace wings in a classicist style, represents a new chapter in history of the Castle. Viennese Nicolo Pacassi was the architect of this re-construction.

A visitor can enter the Castle in three ways. From Hradčanské Square he enters through a ceremonial gate with the giants (by I. F. Platzer) and the first court of honor, where the parades of the Castle Guard made for guests by the republic's president take place. He goes from the first to the second court through an early baroque Matyáš (Mathias) Gate from 1614, which has remained preserved even after Pacassi's construction of the western palace wing. Representative rooms of the president's section can be entered from the passage by going to the right and following the stairway. The left stairway leads to the Spanish Hall through the Columnar

Rosette window of more than 10 meters in diameter in the western portal wall of the main nave of Saint Vitus Cathedral is filled with leaded glass of the World's Creation. It was made in the late 1920's by the glazier J. Vlasák according to the cartoon by F. Kysela. There is an organ auditory beneath the window

Hall, made in the late 1920's by architect J. Plečnik. Worth one's attention is the chapel of Holy Cross with a classicist facade, where the Saint Vitus temple treasure is deposited today, located at the second castle court. A baroque fountain with plastic arts by J. Kohl can be of interest at the court. The Spanish Hall occupies the left part of the northern wing, former Rudolf's stables are located beneath it on the first floor. They have been turned into a picture gallery of Prague Castle. The second court area can be entered through Pacassi Gate as well as over the Powder Bridge across Deer Moat. When looking out of the gate, we see on the left along the road the buil-

PRAGUE CASTLE

dings of former Riding Hall, where a picture gallery is predominantly situated today. Royal gardens and the Summer Palace as well as other beautiful buildings such as the Great Ball House, and in the background toward Mariánská Street the Lion Court, where lions, tigers, and bears were raised, lie on the other side behind the Deer Moat. Even today, a visitor can admire the depth of Deer Moat as well as quality of the Late Gothic fortification above the moat.

There is a passage from the second castle court through the eastern palace wing to the third castle court. An original, Romanesque wall of Soběslav I, reinforced with two towers, used to stand in these places. We can get to the third court from another side too – from Klárov climb the Old Castle Steps, pass

Parades and alternating castle guards at the Court of Honor always attract audiences at the Prague Castle. Both Schwarzenberg palaces located at the southern side of Hradčany Square can be seen in the background behind the gate with statues of fighting giants leading to the court

through a gate near Black Tower and then Jiřská Lane. There is an entrance to the St. Vitus Cathedral, Vladislav Hall with its adjacent rooms, and the president's section from the most spacious, third court. A few dozen meters further we come to Jiřské Square with the basilica of St. George.

St. Vitus Cathedral, whose construction was controlled by the architects Mathias of Arras and Peter Parléř in Charles' times, and completed as it appears today by architects of 19th and 20th century Josef Mocker and Kamil Hilbert, is a dominant feature of the Prague Castle. It is a triple-naved building with one transept, which is entered through the Golden Gate. Above it is a chamber, where the coronation jewels are deposited. The eastern part of the temple along with an adjacent, almost one hundred meters tall tower (which was not completed until the second part of the 16th century and then at the end of the 18th century newly adapted) and

A columnar tower, sticking out from the face of wall, called the Powder or Mihulka Tower, dominates the part of Prague Castle fortification above the Deer Moat. It originated in the Jagellonian period of the castle's reconstruction. Above the other buildings majestically towers the St. Vitus Cathedral

PRAGUE CASTLE

with the related chapels of the choir is the oldest. The most precious chapel of them all – the chapel of St. Václav (Wenceslas) in place of the original rotunda of St. Vitus is located behind the Golden Gate. That is where St. Václav, portrayed by a remarkable limestone statue from 1373, created by Jindřich Parléř, and is located above the altar, was buried after 935. There is access from here to the room, where the coronation jewels are deposited. According to the tradition there are seven keys which open this door. Chapels that originated in Charles' era, stand out in the number of chapels located at the perimeter of the temple. Great leaded glass pieces made according to the designs of outstanding Czech artists – M. Švabinský, K. Svolinský, J. Sequens, C. Bouda, and A. Mucha decorate the windows of all the chapels. Most admired is the window in the Archbishopric Chapel, designed by A. Mucha,

Vladislav Hall occupies the entire area of the Old Royal Palace's third floor. It is the largest secular space of medieval Prague, 62 meters long, 16 meters wide, and 13 meters high. Benedikt Ried of Pístov built it during the reign of Vladislav Jagellonský in 1492–1502. The star-shaped vault of the hall is one of the most admired parts. Five bronze chandeliers hang from its top

illustrating the arrival of the missionaries Cyril and Metoděj (Methode) to the country.

There is an exhibition of twenty-one precious sandstone busts portraying members of the Luxemburg royal family and personalities merited in the construction of the temple, on the walls of a beautiful triforium – a blind columnar arcade. A Royal mausoleum lies in front of the choir. A royal crypt, accessible from the chapel of Holy Cross, is located beneath it. Let us note the Royal Oratory on the right side of the gallery, next to the chapel, which was built during Vladislav Jagellonský's reign.

The main nave with triforium with busts of personalities merited in completion of the temple, built in the

Rider stairway entering the Vladislav Hall is arched by a late Gothic vault designed by Benedikt Ried of Pístov from the period around 1500 and decorated by cross-cut circled ribs. A stairway enabled access to the hall straight from the square in front of St. George basilica even for horses, for there were knightly tilts held in the Vladislav Hall, too

The church of St. George is a triple-naved Romanesque basilica with two characteristic white towers. It got its present appearance from the reconstruction after 1142, thus representing the most preserved monument of the Romanesque period in Prague. Nevertheless, the portal part of the church is from the early baroque period. In the early 18th century built a two-floor baroque chapel of St. John of Nepomuk was built next to it

PRAGUE CASTLE

period of its Neo-Gothic completion, is linked to the medieval Parléř's choir. The western front of the cathedral with two slender towers is monumental. The main entrance is formed by three portals with bronze doors and tympans. There are reliefs with the scenes of the cathedral's history and religious motifs on the doors and tympans. Let us just add the dimensions of the cathedral: length of the temple equals 124 meters, the width of the transept 60 meters, and the height of the main navel's vault is 34 meters.

The triple-naved Romanesque basilica of St. George with two white towers is the second largest temple of the Castle. We'll walk in through the main entrance from Jiřské Square. We can observe the remains of Romanesque paintings from the beginning of the 13th century on an elevated choir with apsis and in the apsis on the left side of the main nave. The tomb of the

The basilica of St. George at the Castle represents a Romanesque jewel of Prague. An elevated choir with apsis, where the remains of Romanesque paintings from the beginning of the 13th century can be found, was connected to the main nave of the church. There, on a stone base rests a wooden painted tomb of the church's founder – the prince Vratislav (at the picture on the left) and also tombstones of the princes Boleslav II and Oldřich

church's founder – prince Vratislav – stands in the area of the main nave. Beneath the choir lies a crypt, whose vaults rest on Romanesque columns from the 12th century. On the southern side of the temple's triple-naved unit we find a columnar portal with tympan, whose relief shows the fight of St. George with a dragon, from the Renaissance period of Benedikt Ried of Pístov's activity. Jiřský Monastery, where the exhibits of the National Gallery are placed connects with the church on its northern side. Pseudo-Gothic building of the New Vicariate and neighboring baroque house of the capitular dean close the northern side of Jiřské Square. From here through a lane we reach the famous restaurant Na Vikárce (At the Vicariate – a note by the translator).

PRAGUE CASTLE

The romantic Golden Lane belongs to the most visited parts of Prague Castle. There, in miniature first-floor houses annexed to the wall above the Deer Moat, the castle shooters and gold-beaters of Rudolf II were living in 16th century. A covered passage, connecting the towers and reinforcing this part of the castle's fortification, runs above the roofs of houses along the wall

Romantic Jiřská Lane between the Jiřské Square and Black Tower is from the square down lined with interesting buildings where used to stand the Rožmberk Palace – the Noblewomen Institution, and the attractive Lobkovický Palace. If we enter the Castle through the gate located in front of the Black Tower, the building of the former residence of the castle's burgrave is on our right side. Daliborka Tower, where according to the legend the prisoner Dalibor of Kozojedy learnt (due to his misery) to play the violin, is accessible over the wall leading from the Black Tower. Daliborka and the other columnar towers White (Bílá) or Powder (Mihulka) originated at the end of the 15th century.

None of the visitors to Prague forgets to see the popular Golden Lane, whose miniature houses, pressed onto the wall above the Deer Moat, created for them-

Majestic impression of St. Vitus Cathedral towering high above the roofs of the surrounding palaces. On the right beneath the castle extends the Lesser Town with its houses, palaces, and gardens. On the left, Hradčany township continues with Schwarzenberg palaces

selves the castle shooters and gold-beaters during the period of Rudolf II.

A walk through the southern gardens of Prague Castle can be an uncommon experience. Architect Josip Plečnik participated in their gorgeous set-up in 1920's. Sense of beauty is multiplied here with grandiose views of Prague and often musical performances, too.

Sight-seeing of Prague Castle with all the historical and cultural monuments available to the visitor will take all day, at least. Changing of the Castle Guard, which serves the Republic's President, will provide a popular spectacle as well. Current President, Václav Havel, gives this famous residence of former rulers, nowadays Presidents of the Czech Republic, proper care.

Prague Castle with St. Vitus Cathedral and a line of palaces from the Terezian period of reconstruction, towers above the roofs of Lesser Town's houses and palaces. We can get a complete picture of Prague from the sightseeing hall on the first floor of the side palace wing, where the representative rooms of the President of the Republic are located

Dominant built-up area of the Loretánské Square: On the left the portal tower of Loreta, in the middle a Capuchin monastery with the church of Angelic Virgin Mary, without a single-naved structure. On the right towers part of the huge Černín Palace, which occupies the entire western part of the square. The palace is the seat of Department of Foreign Affairs of the Czech Republic. In the background on the wooded Petřín hill, a look-out tower soars

HRADČANY

The first settlements on Hradčany ridge west of Prague Castle's mounds can be presumed to have already existed at the beginning of the 11th century, although convincing evidence remains absent. The prince's castle was at that time already a complex with church buildings and bishopric, and was directly influencing the life in its surroundings. Although its closeness had also shady aspects, mainly during enemy attacks, the settlement in Hradčany front fields gradually developed as the demands on services were following the growing importance of the ruler's residence. This way new job opportunities were created, too.

The origin of the serf town of Hradčany dates back to 1320. Its founder was the Prague Castle's burgrave Hynek Berka of Dubá. The small town was partially fortified and enclosed with three gates. The parish church of St. Benedikt, located in the southwestern part of Hradčany Square was already mentioned in writing 1353. As with the other parts of Prague, Hradčany experienced changes which came from the constructional intention of Charles IV. At that time the new walls considerably expanded options for the town's growth. The suburb Pohořelec was founded by the vice-burgrave Aleš of Malkovice west of the original town below the Strahov Monastery in 1375.

During the Hussite revolution Hradčany, as well as the Strahov monastery were afflicted by the conflict between the followers of Zikmund Lucemburský and the Hussites. Frequent fires in the 16th century were disasterous

for the town, too. Nevertheless here, close to the ruler's residence, nobles found, their palaces in the second half of the century. Hradčany town was finally promoted to a king's town by the emperor Rudolf II in 1598. Its citizens created a new town hall in the Renaissance style on Loretánská Street (No. 173). Sgraffiti facade with the remains of the emperor's coat of arms and emblem of the Hradčany town on the portal have remained preserved on the town hall.

Not even during the Thirty Year's War was the town spared of devastating rage of armies. At the same time it came across just how little resistant against the firearms the Gothic walls from the 14th century were. That is why huge baroque bastions were built for this purpose in the second half of the 17th and in the 18th century. They have been preserved in many places (behind the Strahov Monastery, in New World, below streets Na Baště sv. Jiří or Keplerova).

Undoubtedly the most attractive part of Hradčany is the square, from which a view of the western line of the Terezian palaces of Prague Castle with towers of the Saint Vitus Cathedral soaring above them opens up. We can enjoy beautiful views of Prague with the Vltava river, Petřín hill, or the Strahov Monastery from a ramp, located below the Hradčany Square and Prague Castle. Hradčany Square is lined with gorgeous, well-built palaces. Looking from the Castle's Court of Honor, the Archbishop Palace is on our right. However, its last re-

Finely, in rococo style decorated facade of the Archbishop Palace contrasts with the strictness of Saint Vitus Cathedral's towers and rigidity of the Terezian western palace wing of the Prague Castle. The base of the palace is formed by the Renaissance house of Gryspekovský, which was purchased in 1562 by Ferdinand I for the new seat of the renewed Prague's archbishopric

The last reconstruction of the Archbishop Palace at Hradčany Square was realized in 1764–1765 in late baroque style. The facade, however already bears a fine rococo decoration. J. J. Wirch was its architect, Prague's archbishop Antonín Příchovský, whose emblem dominates portal of the palace, was its builder

construction in the style of late baroque from 1764 – 1765 carries on its front facade the elements of tiny rococo style decoration. Šternberk Palace, where some of the exhibits of the National Gallery are placed, lies behind this palace. The western part of the square is formed by the front part of Toskánský Palace, built in the style of Roman baroque. Extensive Schwarzenberg Palace, an outstanding building of Renaissance with sgraffiti and rustics from the 16th century dominates the left, southern side of the square. Today the older military history exhibits are accomodated there. The first classicist palace on the left above the view ramp, originally the palace of Vilém Florentin of Salm, belonged to the Schwarzenbergs since the second half of the 19th century, too. At the end of the left side of the square is St. Benedikt Church with a monastery, and on the right a northern line of buildings terminates the Martinický

Černínská Lane with nice little houses decorated with facades from the 18th and 19th century forms part of the picturesque New World, too. There is a sandstone statue of St. John of Nepomuk from half of the 18th century located on the wall above the house number 97. It was transferred there from Southern Bohemia

Palace, which used to belong to Jaroslav Bořita of Martinice, one of the infamous vice-regents in the events of 1618. Notice the outstanding sgraffito figural decoration on the facade of the palace. In its interior are original decorative elements of Renaissance, too. Today, the center of the square is maintained as a park decorated with an original, free-standing lamp post of the gas lighting from 19th century.

Walking along Loretánská Street, where our attention catches palace No. 177 (Hrzánský), we come to Loretánské Square bordered by Černínský Palace on the western side, the northern part of the square is closed by the church of Angelic Virgin Mary with a former monastery, and the eastern part of the square is dominated by Loreta with a centrally located front tower and Marian chime. Černínský Palace with an adjacent garden

Former Hradčany's suburb New World fascinated a visitor with its rustic atmosphere and peace so contrasting with a nearby rush of the city. Romance emanates from the street corners of New World and Černínská, too. It is as if the time has stopped here, by these low, colorful houses

Strahov premonstrance monastery's complex with the church of Virgin Mary's Ascension represents an inseparable part of Prague's panorama on heights between the Prague Castle and Petřín hill. Today's appearance is after reconstructions of the 17th and 18th century in baroque style, but the church with monastery was founded by king Vladislav II, owing to the initiative of Olomouc's bishop Jindřich Zdík prior to half of the 12th century, already. Remains of the Order's founder, St. Norbert, are deposited in the temple chapel of St. Voršila

was built by Jan and Heřman Černín in the 17th century. The palace was seriously damaged during the French occupation of Prague, but was renewed in the following years under the leadership of architect A. Lurago. Currently it's the seat of the Department of Foreign Affairs of the Czech Republic.

The plain single-naved church of the Angelic Virgin Mary is visited by many residents of Prague especially during the Advent period, when a Nativity scene with life-sized figures can be observed. In contrast to that, Loreta attracts its visitors year-round with the jewelry room, where the diamond monstrance holds superiority. Inside the Loreta complex stands the Santa Casa – Holy Shelter –, copy of a dwelling from Italian Loretto, and the church of Nativity built according to the plans of the father and son Dienzenhofers.

Kapucínská and Černínská Streets descend from Loretánské Square. Both streets lead to a picturesque part of Hradčany, special due to its almost rustic atmosphere –

There is a Philosophical Hall situated in front of the western wall of the convent in an independent building of Strahov Library. The building was erected from 1782–1784 and its classicist portal carries a medallion of Joseph II. The Philosophical Hall is decorated with a ceiling painting called "Humankind History" by the artist A. F. Maulbertsch (end of the 18th century). Books were placed into the baroque shelves, transported over from an abolished premonstratensian monastery in Louka near Znojmo, close to the walls of the hall

to the New World. It originated in the 15th century, its predominantly two storied houses with facades from the 18th and 19th century have been inhabited to this very day, keeping their peace, picturesqueness, and look of a country town with trees stretching from of the gardens. In one of the nice houses is an old popular restaurant "At the Golden Pear". Right around the corner on the street U Kasáren (By the Barracks – a note by the translator) stands the baroque church of St. John of Nepomuk, again in a work by K. I. Dienzenhofer.

From the New World we return to Loretánské Square, where it is just a few steps to Pohořelec (burnt down – a note by the translator). This part of town most likely got its name due to frequent fires. On the left from Lesser Town to Pohořelec climbs the street called Úvoz (hollow way – a note by the translator), above which

HRADČANY

a line of Hradčany's houses, lined from the other side by Loretánská Street, towers. From the opposite ridge this part of Hradčany ressembles the atmosphere of Italian towns built into hillsides. An interesting building of St. Elizabeth hospital from the second half of the 17th century stands in the lower part of Pohořelec above Úvoz. Its facade is dominated by a raised portal above a stairway with a statuary of the Calvary. Southern line of Pohořelec houses closely links with the buildings of former Strahov brewery and ascends all the way to the entrance gate of Strahov Monastery. There, in the upper part of Pohořelec we can still see newly renovated Kučerův Palace, and also "At the Demartins", with an interesting facade. J. J. Wirch, the last archbishop of the Palace, was the author of its design. Pohořelec is enclosed by barracks from the end of the 19th century, built in Neo-Renaissance style. Strahov Gate of Hradčany town used to stand in these places from 1620.

Through the gate in the upper part of Pohořelec we enter the Strahov Monastery. It is decorated by a statue of the founder of the Premonstratensian Order, St. Norbert. Right behind the gate on the left we see the Gothic-Renaissance style church of St. Roch, designed in the beginning of the 17th century by the Italian architect G. M. Fillippi. It was originally the Strahov parish church. Monasterial outbuildings stand behind the church on the left, and buildings of the monasterial library on the right still stand in front of monasterial temple of the Ascension of Virgin Mary. Both halls – Theological and Philosophical – capture visitors' attention due to their decorativeness, quantity and preciousity of the kept volumes and incunabulas. Abbatial temple of the Ascension of Virgin Mary was originally a Romanesque basilica but the reconstructions that took place during the Gothic, Renaissance, and especially baroque period have changed it completely. Strahov Monastery along with the church was built after 1140, when king Vladislav II gave consent for its foundation to the Olomouc's bishop Jindřich Zdík. The monastery itself represents an extensive built-up complex that spreads south and east of the church. It was one of the most important monasteries in Bohemia owing to its extraordinary size and imposing looks, and also scholarship. Rulers were always giving it a lot of attention not only for its cultivated scholarship, but also for defense purposes. It stands in a place favorable for guarding – that's where the name comes from.

The monasterial complex is also part of the panorama of Prague. Between Petřín hill and Prague Castle we notice right away its white buildings and church towers. In contrast, from Strahov Monastery we get a good look of the city and castle even with the gardens and orchards below it, and we can also set off for a walk down to Lesser Town or up to Petřín hill.

The eastern edge of Loretánské Square is dominated by a complex of pilgrim place – the Loreta with a church of Nativity and with a famous belfry at its portal tower. There stands the Santa Casa – a copy of the holy shelter from Italian Loretto – in the middle. A remarkable, so called diamond monstrance, is deposited in the Loretan jewelry room

We can behold the spacious Hradčanské Square, into which Loretánská Street leads, from the height of Saint Vitus Cathedral. There is located Toscana (Toskánský) Palace facing the square. On the left is the beautiful Renaissance Schwarzenberg Palace where the Military History Museum, and the church of St. Benedikt are located today. The Archbishop and Šternberk Palaces are located closest to the Castle. The complex of Strahov Monastery can be seen in the background on the left, as part of the huge portal line of Černín Palace on the right

LESSER TOWN

Lesser Town belongs to one of the most charming parts of Prague. It extends beneath Prague Castle and the slopes of Petřín hill all the way to the Vltava river. The original settlement beneath the castle originated undoubtedly as early as in the late 9th century in connection with the foundation of the Castle. In the oldest chronicles the first notions praising the marketplace, favorable ford across the river – important requirements for a booming trade –, and already appear the Jewish settlement too.

But the real foundation of Lesser Town as a regular king's town with fortifications and related municipal administration does not take place until the period of Přemysl Otakar II's reign. It was Otakar, who in 1257 founded the so called New Town beneath Prague Castle. Later, upon the foundation of Charles's New Town, it was renamed Lesser Town, and finally Little Side. (The English translation for the name of this township remains Lesser Town – a note by the translator.)

The area of present day Lesser Town Square became the central marketplace of Přemysl's town. The road from Judith Bridge, a Romanesque ancestor of the stone Charles Bridge, lead there. Then after connection it continued in the direction of present day Nerudova Street and Újezd toward the castle. Another important communication lead out of the town from a ford located in the area of present day Klárov toward Lesser Town marketplace and then further south up stream. After the significant expansion and new fortification of Lesser Town during Charles IV's reign, the road exited Lesser Town through a gate in the place called Újezd. It remains to this very day. The extensive complex of Gothic Kartouz Monastery, which was later completely destroyed during the Hussite revolution, used to stand there. Charles's new walls enclosed a significant area also on the slopes of Petřín hill (called the Hungry Wall) for the new city and that especially for defense purposes, but also for an optional future construction. Fortunately for modern Prague, these places remained nearly untouched by construction, allowing for the creation of numerous orchards, gardens, and parks. Because of this fact, Lesser Town has been fulfilling the role of a beautiful curative element in Prague's conglomeration. There were two independent administrative territories inside the medieval town. An imposing Gothic episcopal palace used to stand behind Lesser Town's bridge towers on the right between today's Mostecká Street (Bridge Street) and Dražického Square. John IV of Dražice built it. A large garden was extending behind the palace and the complex was enclosed with walls. The residence of Johannines (priestly Order of St. John of Jerusalem) formed an independent administrative complex on the left side of the bridge. Its territory along with

This view of Prague Castle and church of St. Nicholas in Lesser Town is obtainable from the Nostic Palace. It clearly shows how high above the surrounding Lesser Town's buildings the temple's belfry and dome rise. Notice the palace on the left part of the view – it's the Turba Palace at Maltézské Square, built in late baroque style, where the Japanese embassy is located today

Roofs of Lesser Town's houses between Dražického Square and Mostecká Street. In the middle is the torso of one of the former bishopric palace's towers. It used to stand around here since the 14th century. Prague bishop John IV of Dražice was its builder. The palace was destroyed during the Hussite revolution

LESSER TOWN

the church of Virgin Mary below the Chain on the end of the Bridge and palace was enclosed with walls and adhered to an independent jurisdiction as well.

Numerous churches were erected in Lesser Town during the Middle Ages. The previously mentioned Johannine church, municipal parish church of St. Nicholas, and Augustinian church of St. Thomas with monastery belonged to the most significant ones. To this kind of historical monuments belongs also St. John at Laundry Chapel built in the early Gothic style, which was along with the settlement Újezd included within the Charles's walls. These walls descended the slopes of Petřín hill down to the Vltava river in

Dominative feature of Lesser Town (the temple of St. Nicholas) can be found at nearly all postcards of Lesser Town. Its green dome towers from all sides above the other houses and palaces. Lighted New Castle Steps will take us in a while from the Castle all the way to a jewel of Renaissance – the palace of lords of Hradec

line with today's Vítězná Avenue (meaning Victorious – a note by the translator). There, in the yard of house number 531 we can still see the remains of the walls. Notice the remarkable neo-Renaissance and classicist architecture of the houses located at Vítězná Avenue. The avenue leads to the bridge of Legions, across which we come to the National Theatre.

The boom in Charles IV's era brought forth Lesser Town as well, too, but the following stage meant nearly a complete disaster for the town. It became a cruel battlefield between the Catholics of Prague Castle and Hussites right at the beginning of the Hussite revolution. The town was burnt down several times. Most houses and churches were damaged. As the writers of old chronicles state, wild animals were

The interior of St. Nicholas Church represents an admired example of the splendour of baroque at its zenith in Prague. The sculptor I. F. Platzer created between 1752 – 1755 the huge statues of saints located in front of the pillars, while artist F. X. Balko decorated the church with frescos. The giant statues of Church Teachers from 1769 and the altar statue of St. Nicholas were created by I. F. Platzer as well

Church of Virgin Mary below the Chain located by a former Johannine monastery, was founded as a Romanesque basilica. Reconstruction in the 14th century was not completed, and its existence is evidenced only by two robust prismatic towers. Between them the church, adapted at the break of the 16th and 17th century, can be entered through the front yard. The appearance of the church today is the result of baroque reconstruction by the architect C. Lurago

Gardens and orchards covering the slopes of Petřín hill are a much sought-after relaxation place of rest and walks. Even from here we can enjoy interesting views of Prague Castle and the built-up part of Lesser Town

running across the streets of the destroyed town. Not until the reign of Hussite king George of Poděbrady did Lesser Town recover from its wounds. An original Romanesque bridge tower was repaired, and in place of the other arose a new one, built in late Gothic style. This is how Lesser Town's bridge termination gained its way its distinctive appearance, (characteristic twin tower with a gate located in the middle). This appearance has remained preserved. The town, however, had not enjoyed its peace for a long time, because in the course of the 16th century it was disturbed by many disasterous fires. The biggest one of them in 1541 turned most of Lesser Town into ash and got carried over to Hradčany and Prague Castle. However, destruction of the old buildings paradoxically left the space open for new construction, this time in the spirit of Renaissance which mainly the nobles took

advantage of. The Renaissance palace of the Smiřický family has been a characteristic feature of the northern part of Lesser Town Square up to the present day. In between the Castle Steps and Nerudova Street dominates the palace of lords of Hradec.

However, Lesser Town did not experienced the greatest improvement until the baroque period. Soon after the Thirty Year's War, which wasted the town again, outstanding Italian, German, Czech, and other architects in service of the broad-minded builders who came of the post-White mountain's period nobility, got to work at still vacant places, or for a bargain purchased plots destroyed by the fire. Albrecht of Valdštejn was the first of these builders. His huge

LESSER TOWN

palace, garden, and other related properties absorbed the plots where dozens of houses used to be (construction as early as 1623–1629). Among other outstanding palace buildings from the 17th and 18th century are for example the Nostic Palace (at the Maltese Square), Buquoy (at the Velkopřevorské Square), Kaiserštejn at Kampa, Thun-Leslie (Thun Street), Schönborn (Tržiště Street), Lobkovic (Vlašská Street), Lichtenštejn and Kaiserštejn (Lesser Town Square) or Thun-Hohenštejn Palace (Nerudova Street). The gardens, located on the slopes beneath Prague Castle, belonging to the palaces: Pálffy, Kolovrat, Černín or Fürstenberk (Valdštejnská Street), and Vrtba below Petřín hill are also excellent horticultural compositions as well as architectural pieces. We can enjoy music in the pictures-

Unparalleled views of Prague Castle with St. Vitus Cathedral present themselves from Valdštejnská Street. The terraced palace gardens with stairways, bowers balustrades, and fountains ascend the Castle behind the palaces lining the right side of Valdštejnská Street. The baroque facade with classicist elements belongs to Kolowrat Palace, Valdštejn Palace is across the street

que, peaceful environment of frequent concerts which take place in some of the palace gardens. The seat of the Czech Assembly has been located in Thun Palace on Sněmovní Street since 1812. Due to this tradition, the parliament of the republic was placed there as well. Some of the other palaces in Lesser Town serve as the seats of various departments or foreign embassies.

Baroque architecture used its sense of richness and pomposity on church buildings, especially temples. St. Nicholas temple, whose giant dome and belfry rise high above Lesser Town's roofs, represents an inseparable part of Prague's panorama. Thanks to the care of the Jesuits, it has gone through an extensive reconstruction. Its builders, father and son Dienzenhofers along with Anselmo Lurago, created the most characteristic building of Prague baroque. The other huge buildings, which were used by the

Valdštejn Palace with adjacent outbuildings, riding hall, and garden represents an area which, due to its spaciousness and showiness, could compete with Prague Castle. The palace, along with its famous sala terrena, was built for Albrecht of Valdštejn according to the plans of Italian architects. Walks through the palace garden with a man-made pond, the cave with stalactites, and the views of Prague Castle are unforgettable

The view from the Old Town Bridge Tower offers a unique experience to the visitors of Prague. Ancient Charles Bridge, which has for centuries been main Prague's communication, leads toward Lesser Town's bridge towers and links both banks of the Vltava river. Lesser Town's temple of St. Nicholas is the center of attention, and Strahov Monastery lies to the left of it on heights. Saint Vitus Cathedral of Prague Castle is located to the right of it, forming a quite typical panorama of Prague

LESSER TOWN

Jesuit order as a high school, among other purposes, are connected to the temple. The St. Thomas Church (Letenská Street) or the church of Victorious Virgin Mary (Karmelitská Street) with a remarkable waxy statue of the little Jesus of Prague have also gone through reconstruction. Newly built were for example the church of St. Joseph (Josefská Street) or church of Virgin Mary of Constant help (Nerudova Street).

Also the island of Kampa, which today, due to its parks and wonderful views of the river, bridges, and Old Town embankment attracts visitors as well as the locals for a walk gradually experienced changes during the late baroque period. Another much sought-after place is the charming „Lesser Town's Venice". Its houses get washed by the arm of the Vltava river

The island of Kampa, located in the very centre of the city, is a place of green oasis and places of frequent strolls and relaxation. The entire southern part of the island is maintained as a park with grassy areas. Following the stairway and then further beneath the tenement houses along Lesser Town's short embankment we shortly reach the bridge of Legions and then the National Theatre

A somewhat unusual look across the Vltava and its bridges. In the distance on a rock, towers the church of St. Peter and Paul at Vyšehrad. We see the built-up part of Lesser Town in the front between the higher bridge tower and Letenská Street, where the archbishop's garden used to stretch out

called Čertovka (place where the devils rage – a note by the translator) which separates the island of Kampa from the river. Also the Great Abbot's Mill with an admired millstone running on lower race contributes to the romance of the place.

Fortunately, during the period of Prague's industrialization and demolition, Lesser Town basically preserved its original appearance. This township is currently experiencing quite fundamental renovations of its palaces, gardens, and houses, but remains the most beautiful part of the capital. Not only can the visitor enjoy the old architecture every step of his way, but he can also enjoy the picturesque street and lane corners, or breath in some fresh air in the parks, gardens, and orchards. The walk can be tied to entertainment visiting either on foot or by cable railway the wooded Petřín hill and seeing the look-out tower or mirror-labyrinth located there.

A characteristic silhouette of Charles Bridge's Lesser Town termination – the twin-tower with a gate, and behind them the temple of St. Nicholas. The lower Romanesque tower originated towards the end of the 12th century, while the higher one was built during the reign of George of Poděbrady. Mostecká Street leads from the gate to Lesser Town Square

OLD TOWN

Prague's Old Town is inseparably tied to the history of the whole Czech land. It has always been the most important and richest town, leaning on the extraordinary favor of Czech rulers throughout most of its existence. It has been a respected leader of other Czech towns. Problems of the entire kingdom were sometimes solved at its town hall when there was no appointed king.

The first settlements at the location of the future town appeared in the Prague basin on the right bank of the Vltava river near trails that lead to the fords across the river. They were mercantile settlements, but gradually also first craftsmen and people seeking subsistence began settling here, at an important trading place near the prince's castle, too. Not only Czechs were concentrated in this area. So did German merchants, or people of Romanic origin, and Jews, who very quickly had their own settlement here with a synagogue on the left bank's lower castle. Consolidating the power of the Přemysl dynasty secured safety and possibilities of an economic boom to this settlement. So as the rulers were paying greater attention to Vyšehrad, the populated area was expanding towards this second prince's castle. This fact has been reflected in the name of the settlement itself, being called Mezihradí (meaning an area between two castles – a note by the translator). The real founding of the town, along with all respective signs such as fortification, municipal authority and referring jurisdiction, took place later, in the 13th century. King Václav I initiated fortification of the town after 1230. Thus not only militarily securing its undisturbed development, but simultaneously taking an important step towards uniting a community, which had been, until then, scattered in this area. The fortification belt of this new town was 1,700 metres long, enclosing an area of 140 hectars. The fortification was reinforced by a number of towers and a deep moat, while the entrance to town was guarded with gates.

Conversion to a real town was completed under the reign of king Václav II, when a twelve-member consul administration headed the town and a royal officer controlled it. However, John Lucemburský was he one who issued the document in 1338 in Amiens allowing the citizens to create a town hall. This way the king rewarded the citizens for irrevocable loans provided by them for his costly international policies. The Old Town hall became accepted place for government and administration of the town and many significant decisions often influencing the run of events of the entire kingdom were made inside its walls in the course of the following centuries.

An unusual boom Old Town (as Prague town or Greater Town of Prague was called behind its walls when New Town was founded) achieved in times of Charles IV and also in the beginning of his son's reign. The founding of Charles University, construction of the

This part of Old Town is dominated by a tall towery portal of the burgess cathedral of Virgin Mary before Týn. In the background on the left soars the tower of another Old Town church – St. Jacob. On the right stretches the huge tower of Old Town Hall. There are the following houses in front of the Týnský temple: on the left the towery house At the Stone Bell from the 14th century (the period of John Lucemburský's reign), Týn School with Renaissance portal gables from the second half of the 16th century, and the house At the White Unicorn. The Art Nouveau building of New Town Hall at Mariánské Square is located closest to us

Renowned astrological clock, placed at the Old Town Hall's tower, was made for town already in the beginning of the 15th century by the clockmaker Mikuláš of Kadaň. It was perfected at the end of the century by master Hanuš. The astrological clock consists of two parts: The circular sphere measures the time and shows the movement of Sun around the Earth, a calendar with paintings by J. Mánes motivated by life of the rural people is placed beneath it. Moving apostles appear in the window every hour to the joy of little as well as the adult visitors.

Western line of Pařížská Street's eclectic and Art Nouveau tenement houses with numerous gables, towers, and spires proves that Prague is a hundred-spired city. Even the towers and dome of the baroque temple of St. Nicholas, located at the Old Town Square, and the Gothic tower of Old Town Hall prove this fact

entire campus, construction of a new stone bridge with a monumental bridge tower, town hall complex, re-structuring, and building churches belonged to the most significant events of those times. Neither did the town citizens, especially the mercantile patricians, lag behind in construction activity. That is why the town became a truely dignified center of the Czech kindom and pride of the Roman king in this period.

The decline of the political importance of the Czech state during the reign of Václav IV and the fact that Prague has not been a residential town of the Roman king since 1400, fatefully reflected on prosperity of Old Town, too. Consequently problems of a religious and social nature worsened, what's more, the country suffe-red with epidemics. Answers and solutions were sought to resolve these woeful phenomena. Some of the mas-ters of Prague University stepped behind the " legal" li-ne of research. Outstanding thinkers of the Czech nati-on such as John Huss, Jeroným of Prague, or Jakoubek (little Jacob – a note by the translator) of Stříbro, des-cended from its intellectual environment. Thus the University became a scientific base from which the re-formation movement leading toward correction of the

disorders in church and consequently in society drew. It was just Jakoubek of Stříbro, who initiated, upon con-sulting Huss (who has then already imprisoned in Konstanz) an Utraquist communion in the church of St. Martin in the Wall in Old Town.

Prague was the heart of Hussite Bohemia during the Hussite revolution. Hussite allies were making impor-tant military decisions to protect the country at the Old Town Hall. They discussed there matters of faith, and sent from there delegations abroad. This historic period culminated in the election of a Czech Utraquist noble George of Poděbrady for Czech king in the main hall of the Old Town Town Hall in 1458.

Also in the following period of Jagellon family reign in Bohemia the Old Town maintained an important role at contemporary scene due to the fact that the central power was not strong. The town also prospered econo-mically, which was reflected even on new constructions and reconstructions (Old Town Hall) of administrative, church, and civic properties in the spirit of late, so cal-led Jagellon Gothic.

Participation in the anti-Habsburg uprising in 1547 and 1619 ended unhappily for the Old Town. Back then

Portal part of the Old Town Hall's buildings is admired by all visitors of Prague. The astrological clock with apostles enjoys the greatest attention, but the late Gothic and Renaissance decoration of the town hall's buildings, especially the Renaissance window with a sign reading PRAGA CAPUT REGNI reclives the same source of admiration. Renaissance house called At the Minute with gorgeous figural sgraffiti comes forward on the left

Old-New Synagogue, located in the lower part of Maiselova Street in Jewish Town and built after 1270, is the most precious local monument. Opposite it, separated only by narrow Červená Lane, stands the town hall of Jewish Town with a hebrew clock placed at its gable and a little tower. The town hall got its present appearance in the second half of the 18th century following a reconstruction of the original building, constructed at the expense of M. Maisel at the end of the 16th century

OLD TOWN

the town lost a number of its privileges after being defeated, and many citizens were badly afflicted given the death penalty or exile. Because of this pressure, at the end of the Thirty Year's War the Old Town was already loyally standing at the side of the Habsburgs. Its walls were protected against the attacks of the Swedish armies by citizens, students, as well as Jews.

The appearance of the town was strongly affected by baroque. Many magnificent temples were erected here. The most noted one is St. Nicholas at the Old Town Square (designed by K. I. Dienzenhofer). In baroque style was restructured the St. Jacob and St. Havel churches as well as many others. The Order of Merciful Brothers built an extensive hospital and monastery complex with Simon and Juda Church (on the river bank Na

The Old Jewish Cemetery is one of the most visited Prague's monuments. There are approximately 12,000 tombstones. The oldest preserved tombstone of Avigdor Karo originated in 1439. Some of the most significant personalities of the Jewish Town buried here are: the rabbi Löw, according to the legend the creator of a man-made person (Golem), and primas and patron Mordechaj Maisel

Františku). An even larger construction complex in Old Town originated in the front fields of Charles Bridge through the care of the Jesuits (Klementinum) with a library and observatory, and St. Salvátor with St. Kliment churches. Their palaces built in Old Town the nobility as well. A visitor can see the most beautiful and significant of them at the Old Town Square – the Golz-Kinský Palace, in Husova street the Clam-Gallas Palace, in Celetná Street the palaces of Hrzán of Harasov, Pachta of Rájov, and Millesimovský or Colloredo-Mansfeld Palaces on Charles Street. Not even the patritians laggen behind and they either restructured their houses from their foundation, or added to their dwellings at least a baroque facade. Stone Charles Bridge received a magnificent rare decoration, for the most well-known artists, such as M. B. Braun, M. V. Jäckel, F. M. Brokoff or J. O. Mayer and others, gradually re-created it in a sculptural gallery in the open.

Pleasing view of the Vltava river with its bridges. In front is the Mánesův, behind it Charles Bridge and others. Closest are the roofs of buildings of the Cabinet Office complex, on the left part is Alšovo Embankment. The tall, green dome belongs to the church of St. František at Křížovnické Square. Further stands the Old Town Bridge Tower, Old Town's mills with tower, and behind them the building of the National Theatre

OLD TOWN

An extensive demolition took place in the late 19th century in parts of the Old Town as well as in Jewish Town – a part of the Old Town. Some historically precious buildings were sacrificed for this reason. New streets with gorgeous, mostly tenement houses, built in historicizing styles and Art Nouveau, were erected at the demolished sites. Today, they are considered architectural gems of the city (special attention deserves especially Maiselova, Široká, Kaprova, Vězeňská, V Kolkovně, and Kozí streets). Completely demolished was part of the town lying near the river and separated from it by a high embankment – a place to stroll for Prague residents as well as for its visitors. There are great views of the Castle, Petřín hill, Lesser Town, and Prague's bridges from the Old Town river banks. These views yield unforgettable experiences.

The Old Town Square with Town Hall, astrological clock, and monumental memorial of master John Huss, built in Art Nouveau style, is the natural center of the town where historical events took place. The spacious square is dominated by a lofty portal of the municipal Gothic cathedral of Virgin Mary before Týn. From there we can admire rows of magnificent houses on Pařížská Boulevard, which leads to a remarkable bridge built in the Art Nouveau style – the Svatopluk Čech Bridge.

We can recommend to those interested in history to visit the Anežský Monastery complex " Na Františku".

This precious monument was already founded in the 13th century. From Pařížská (Paris – a note by the translator) Boulevard we enter the Jewish Town directly. Its Staronová (Old-New – a note by the translator) Synagogue from the second half of the 13th century and the Old Jewish Cemetery have been admired by visitors from all over the world.

Noted Czech architects, sculptors, and art-oriented craftsmen created at the begining of the 20th century the Community House, built in Art Nouveau style. The King's Court used to be located in its place. Since Václav IV time till the Prague residents' riots in 1483, it was a frequent residence of the kings. A huge, neo-Gothically modified Prašná (Powder – a note by the translator) Gate towers near it. We reach these points of interest after a few minutes walk from the Old Town Square through Celetná Street. We notice a cubistic jewel – the house " At the Black Madonna". No visitor should miss the walk along the route of the former municipal moats, especially the streets Na Příkopě, Na Můstku, and Národní, which are truely live metropolitan arteries. We can view Wenceslas Square from Můstek and in of subway station we can see the remains of a little Gothic bridge above the Old Town moat. (Meanings of the names Na Příkopě, Na Můstku, and Národní are: At the Moat, At the Little Bridge, and National – a note by the translator).

Mayoral Lounge, vaulted with a fiat dome with A. Mucha's paintings placed in a central circle, three lunettes, and sectors belongs to the most admired of all halls of the Community House. Mucha's paintings here, on well-known personalities of the Czech history, praise the common civic virtues

The church of St. Nicholas, located at the Old Town Square, designed the prominent creator of the Prague's baroque – K. I. Dienzenhofer. It was built between 1732–1735. Statues created by A. Braun decorate its southern front with main portal and two towers. The church, through its baroque lines, makes a remarkable antipode to the Gothic Týnský temple, located at the opposite side of the square

A unique, open–air gallery of Charles Bridge makes almost a mystic impression in the morning sunrise. It is formed by statues and statuaries of saints, made by outstanding sculptors of the baroque era up to the creators of the 19th century. The huge Bridge Tower from the second half of the 14th century represents an entrance to the Old Town. The magic of the view is multiplied by the robust dome of the church of St. František and towers of the St. Salvátor Church above Křížovnické Square, located behind the bridge

NEW TOWN

In 1348 Charles IV founded the New Town of Prague. A space behind the walls in a wide belt between Vyšehrad and the bank of the Vltava river near the settlement Poříčí at northern side, beside settlements Opatovice, Rybníček, Podskalí, and others expected to become part of New Town of Prague, was given for this purpose. The town's planned area was about 360 ha (an area more than double in size compared to the first town of Prague).

The newly constructed walls were over 3 km long (there were no walls facing Old Town and Vyšehrad, built indeed), harmonized by square defense towers, but the gates were preponderant: the Peter Gate at Poříčí and Mountain Gate, from which the road to Kutná Hora lead, at the end of today's Hybernská Street. St. Prokop Gate, also called the Horse Gate, used to stand in place of today's National Museum. It functioned as the entrance to the second largest New Town's area – the Horse Market. Through largest gate of St. John as well as the Swine Gate people entered the largest New Town's open-air market – the Cattle Market, called Charles Square (Karlovo náměstí) these days, in the direction of today's Ječná Street. The third largest area was the Hay Market, today's Senovážné Square (meaning transporting hay – a note by the translator) where the trading of grains and hay used to take place.

Since the very beginning, construction followed a thought out plan in plotting the entire area, as well as in building up the designated township. The streets were layed, and construction of individual houses was executed according to the regulations. The ruler himself supposedly oversaw the work. That's why one of the streets, which originated unintentionally, has been bearing the name Nekázanka (possesing the lack of discipline – a note by the translator) up to the present day. New Gothic temples and monasteries monumentally towered over the town representing a God-loving ruler as well as the power of the catholic church. Perhaps most remarkable is Augustinian church located at the fortification belt's corner high above the Nusle Valley across from Vyšehrad at a location called At Karlov (well-known star-shaped vault originated later in the second half of the 16th century) or monasterial church of the Benediktin Order of Slavic liturgy in Emauzy above the road to Vyšehrad.

New Town has developed quite independently of the first town of Prague. It had its own consuls (12) with a mayor and supervising royal officer – rychtář. Soon they even built a town hall at the Cattle Market.

New Town has been ever since its foundation rather a center of craftsmen and poorer town classes. Because of this fact, trades that might have been noi-

Wavy facades of rows of houses line the Masaryk Embankment. The houses were built at the beginning of the 20th century, and neo-Gothic, neo-Renaissance, neo-baroque and the Art Nouveau styles were used on its facades on a wide scale. Attention should be given to the Art Nouveau house No. 224 by the architect J. Stibral with a rich sculptural decoration by L. Šaloun, or the house No. 248 built by J. Fanta between 1903–1905 for the Prague singing club Hlahol

National Theatre, the most beautiful work of the 19th century architecture, rises above the surrounding buildings opposite of Lažanský Palace, which ends the row of buildings on the Smetana Embankment. The theatre developed by collecting pieces from the whole nation between 1868–1881. Right after its completion it burnt down, but in 1883 it was reopened. The theatre was designed in the style of the late North Italian neo-Renaissance by architect J. Zítek. Completion, following the fire, was handled by J. Schulz

NEW TOWN

sy or odorsome to the densely populated Old Town, were supposed to be concentrated there.

The coexistence of many towns in Prague has had a lot of problems since the beginning. They were not eliminated by occassional attempts for administrative connection into a single unit in 1784, either.

The town entered the Czech history through events that took place on July 30, 1419. On that day Hussite priest John Želivský brought a discontented crowd from sermon in the church of Virgin Mary of Snow (which was assigned to the adherents of the chalice – Hussites) under the windows of New Town Hall, where he demanded the release of imprisoned Hussites. When the only response from the consuls in town hall was ridicule and even stone throwing, a raging crowd took the town hall by storm. They threw the consuls down onto spears and gained the upper hand over the town hall as well as the town itself. A high-ranking royal officer with his mercenaries arrived to bring order, but he became scared by the armed crowd and withdrew. Eventually king Václav IV reluctantly acknowledged the pro-Hussite takeover in New Town by confirming the consuls picked by the people. That day is considered to the beginning of the Hussite revolution.

A considerable part of New Town remained nearly undeveloped till the end of the 19th century. That is why at many marginal locations, especially in the direction toward Vyšehrad and above the Nusle Valley, gardens, vineyards, and orchards owned by patricians and nobility thrived. Many baroque churches and monasterial complexes were added to the numerous magnificent church buildings from Charles's era, whose part, however, was damaged during the Hussite period. The most extensive one along with the church of St. Ignác was built by the Jesuits on the eastern side of Cattle Market. Above the road to Vyšehrad, opposite the Gothic church in Emauzy, was erected a baroque church of St. John of Nepomuk according to the design of K. I. Dienzenhofer. It is noted for its towered portal. Somewhat further up the street Na Slupi, the same architect designed the monasterial church of Virgin Mary for the Elisabeth Order. The buildings of a monastery and hospital were adjacent to it. This famous architect then collaborated on a temple project on Resslova Street with P. I. Bayer. This temple is known for being the hiding place of a Czechoslovak parachutists after the assassination of Deputy Reich Protector

Panteon – the national sanctuary, dedicated to the memory of great personalities of the nation, represents the most important part of the National Museum. The square space with galleries is vaulted by a dome and decorated with four paintings on its walls, which represent important events of the Czech history. V. Brožík is the author of mural paintings of the Foundation of Charles University (facing at the picture) and J. A. Komenský in Amsterodam (on the left). He painted them in 1898

National Museum, dominant feature of Wenceslas Square, is located at its upper end. It was built between 1885–1890 according to the design of architect J. Schulz in the style of then fashionable neo-Renaissance. The main portal front of the museum, which is more than 100 meters long is imposing especially in the central part of the wing leading to the square. The gallery of the National Museum provides a popular view of the entire Wenceslas Square

NEW TOWN

R. Heydrich as well as the place where they lost their lives after an unequal struggle. The temple belongs to the Orthodox Church these days, and it is dedicated to St. Cyril and Methode. An interesting baroque complex was built for the Order of Voršila near the moat separating both towns in the area of today's Národní Avenue close to the National Theatre.

The nobility built its palaces in vacant areas or in the places of old development. The palace of Losa of Losinthal on today's Hybernská Street (the so-called People's House, today the headquarters of the Czech Social Democratic Party) is one of the most extensive ones. The street bears the name of monks of Irish origin who had their monastery opposite the Powder Gate (Tower). The original monasterial building was adapted to the classicist style in the beginning of the 19th century. The Sylva-Tarouccy Palace on the stre-

Hotel Evropa, whose design and construction was shared by the architects B. Bendelmayer and A. Dryák, is the most beautiful building constructed in the Art Nouveau style at Wenceslas Square. Nymphs surrounding a lantern dominate the house above its front gable with a gilded sign and colorful mosaic by J. Förster. A peacock, typical for the Art Nouveau decorativeness is not missing, either. Sculptor L. Šaloun is the author of this allegoric group

et Na Příkopech is a gem of baroque. The Mladota of Solopysky Palace in the southern part of Charles Square is rather known under the name Faust's House, because it is tied to the legend of doctor Faust. The story goes that, one of the Mladotas perfomed some chemical laboratory testing there. Alchemist Edward Kelley was residing in the house, which used to be here in the 16th century. Also much sought-after is the chateau of Michna of Vacínov (Ke Karlovu Street), where the memorial of the world-famous Czech composer Antonín Dvořák is located).

The current appearance of New Town is to a considerable extent not only the result of Charles's era or

Wenceslas Square forms today the largest boulevard, nearly 700 meters long, and 60 meters wide. It is a place of busy commercial and social life, but also the setting, where important political events have been taking place. There is the rider statue of St. Václav, placed in the upper part of the square. Houses and palaces built mostly in the 19th and 20th century line both sides of the square. In many cases the seats of banks, commercial companies, hotel facilities, and stores are located there

NEW TOWN

baroque influence, but also of an unusual boom in construction activity in the second half of the 19th, and in the beginning of the 20th century. It had to happen due to the industrial and commercial development and release from the shell of walls. Railroad transportation was developing as well, and railway station complexes were developing on the perimeter of the town. Nowadays they are interesting architectural monuments – as for example the classicist Masaryk Station or Main Station, built in the Art Nouveau style. The building of the National Theatre in neo-Renaissance style can be noted as a distinguished, lately erected building whose importance extended beyond the town. It was built from the yield of the national collection. The National Museum, located the upper part of Wenceslas Square, whose palaces and houses representative of Czech architecture from the 19th and 20th century, has a similar importance for the Czech nation. Especially outstanding is the Art Nouveau hotel Evropa (Europe) and complex of buildings Lucerna (Lantern) or the corner palace Koruna (Crown). An interesting complex of hospital buildings and Prague's maternity hospital was erected in the upper part of New Town between Karlov and the church of St. Apolinář. A grandiose construction has taken place in the demolished parts of town, especially in the flood endangered areas. Such fundamental changes occurred in the part of town located south of the National Theatre in the area surrounding the St. Vojtěch Church or at Poříčí. The part of town in neighbourhood of the Senovážné Square was also demolished. Not far from here, on Jeruzalémská Street, Jews built the Jubilee Synagogue in Mauro-Art Nouveau style. The construction of the embankment along the entire length of the Vltava bank was completed in the beginning of the 20th century. At the same time, a row of ostentatious rental houses with facades of various historical styles was erected along the stretch from the National Theatre toward Vyšehrad. Quite outstanding, however, are the Art Nouveau houses along the stretch between the National Theatre and Jiráskovo Square (more detailed information is provided in the book Prague and the Art Nouveau, published by the V Ráji Publishing House in Prague).

The most busy place of New Town since the Middle Ages has been Wenceslas Square (former Horse Market). It witnessed every social, national, and political event in the course of the 19th and 20th century because the Czech nation here, near patron of the country – St. Václav (Wenceslas), – symbolized by the rider statue by J. V. Myslbek, located in the upper part of the square –, sought instinctively or purposefully support and refuge.

Church of Virgin Mary of the Snow is the highest church building in Prague. It was founded by Charles IV in 1347. It never got completed, however. Current large building with a 33 meter high vault, represents a mere presbytery of an unrealized plan of a triple-naved temple's building. Imposing, late Renaissance vault originated in the beginning of the 17th century, when the church was handed over to the possession of Franciscan Order. The temple can be entered from Jungmann Square

Legendary Vyšehrad rock with a part of the Gothic and baroque fortification.
The remains of the Gothic watch-house are, according to people interpretation,
called Libuše's bath. A view of Prague is available from the corner of the
baroque bastion. The slender neo-Gothic towers belong to the church
of St. Peter and Paul, which gained its appearance following
the reconstruction at the break of the 19th and 20th century

VYŠEHRAD

The legendary castle Vyšehrad, (high castle – note by the translator) the residence of the first Czech rulers mentioned in old tales, is located on a bluff, which falls steeply at its western rocky end down to the current of the Vltava river. Old Czech legends suggest that the castle was the oldest residence of the legendary princess Libuše, who foretold the founding of Prague and the future of the country from the castle of Vyšehrad. Nevertheless, the initiation of the local castle site has been traced back to the first half of the 10th century. Thus the prince's castle is undoubtedly newer than Prague Castle. In spite of that Vyšehrad was for a period of time a renowned prince's and even royal palace. During the reign of Boleslav II, as the found denars show, even a mint was in operation and Vyšehrad was already a Přemysl dynasty castle site protected by fortifications at that time. There were stone and wooden buildings of a secular as well as religious nature standing inside. The castle enjoyed the importance of an administration center during the reign of Přemysl dynasty princes Vratislav II (who was crowned as the first Czech king) Konrád, and Soběslav I. The extensive construction activity bears witness to the importance and care given to Vyšehrad by the Přemysl family. In 1070, the Vyšehrad abbey, independent of Prague's bishop, was founded. Subsequently, the Romanesque basilica of St. Peter and Paul was founded too. A precious illuminated book, so called Coronation kodex was written there in 1085 for the king Vratislav I as well.

At the end of the 12th and in the course of the 13th century the rulers had already permanently resided at Prague Castle. Vyšehrad had remained the seat of abbey only so its importance declined. Only later, Charles IV, son of the Czech king John Lucemburský, a Přemysl dynasty descendant after his mother Eliška, renewed the faded glory of Vyšehrad. He initiated construction in the spirit of contemporary architectural fashion. The ruler's ideas of dignity of the residence for the Czech kings were subsequently realized. New houses for the ruler as well as the administration and religious buildings, and particularly perfect fortification done according to contemporary fortification rules, made Vyšehrad a modern habitation, religious and military complex towering for the defense of New Town south of it above Vltava and valley of the Botič creek.

The uniqueness of the fortification zoned by towers was accented by a huge gate – passage fortress –, from which the road from Prague going through Vyšehrad continued further to Southern Bohemia. The gate, later

Slavín, a common vault of the most merited men and women of the Czech nation, dominates the Vyšehrad cemetery in the middle of its eastern side. It was built between 1889–1890 from the initiative of burgess P. Fišer and Vyšehrad's dean M. Karlach. Slavín was designed by the architect A. Wiehl. J. Mauder was the author of sculptural decoration in 1892–1893

Northern arcade of the Vyšehrad cemetery originated according to the design of the architect of Czech neo-Renaissance A. Wiehl in the last decade of the 19th century. The grave of the Czech composer Antonín Dvořák with a bust by the master of Czech Art Nouveau L. Šaloun is particularly frequently visited

VYŠEHRAD

called Špička, (meaning a point – a note by the translator) is highly noticeable at veduta from 1562, for it overcame the devastation of the original Charles's Vyšehrad. On the contrary, it was adapted during the late Gothic period. It did not outlive the baroque adaptations, however. Also the second main gate on the Prague side, thus called Prague or Jerusalem Gate, was a huge one. It was probably properly decorated because the coronation procession of the Czech kings heading through Prague towns on Royal Way over a stone bridge to the Prague castle, was supposed to exit from there.

In the course of the Hussite revolution Vyšehrad was besieged by the Prague residents and their allies. However, the fortress was impregnable, and starving

Capitular and parish church of St. Peter and Paul at Vyšehrad. Today's appearance represents a synthesis of Gothic triple-naved unit from the 14th century and a neo-Gothic main nave, choir and front from the turn of the 19th and 20th century. The interior is predominantly neo-Gothic and Art Nouveau, painting of Virgin Mary of the Rain from the 14th century and a Romanesque tomb, assumed to represent St. Longin, from the beginning of the 12th century, are the most precious exhibits

the crew out presented the only option. When Zikmund Lucemburský, the successor to the throne, rejected by the Hussites, finally came to the rescue, he did not get the expected support of the starved mercenaries from the castle. The crew signed a truce in the meantime and, according to it, remained idle during the course of the battle so that Zikmund was terribly defeated in front of the castle's fortifications. The Hussites then allowed honorable departure for the crew, but destroyed the fortification of the side facing the town so that Vyšehrad could have presented no danger to the town anymore. Many administration and religious buildings were damaged or completely destroyed indeed.

The reconstruction of Vyšehrad as a huge baroque citadel represents a significant chapter in its history. After the woeful experiences of the Thirty Year's War Vyšehrad was supposed to be a guarantee of the city's defense from enemy actions lead from the South and Southeast. The fortress was constructed according to

S6 · MARIA · ORA · PRO · NOBIS

The interior of St. Peter and Paul temple captures one's attention with an ostentatious Art Nouveau painting, motivated by Czech history, its saints and rulers. Also the floral motives and ornaments made in folk style are gorgeous. Husband and wife Urban were authors of these paintings between 1902–1903

the plans of military fortification builders, who were represented by Inocenc Conti and Joseph Priami since 1654. Even today huge masonry baroque fortifications raise expert's admiration in spite of the fact that the original plans involving also the fortification construction of the Botič valley, Capitular Island, and the opposite bank of the Vltava river were not realized. The fact is that the fortress never saved the city. Quite the contrary, it served the occupation by French (who built casemates there in 1741–1742) and by further Prussian armies (1744).

A visitor unacquainted with Prague will best reach the castle by taking the subway to the Vyšehrad station and from there, after a few minutes, will enter the

Plaque painting of the Virgin Mary of the Rain, set on an altar in the third chapel on the right, stands out in the Vyšehrad temple of St. Peter and Paul. It originated in the period around 1350. It is an exceptional work of Czech Gothic art. The painting used to be displayed in the Church of Humility of the Virgin Mary under Vyšehrad

fortress through the baroque Táborská Gate. Soon he will pass by the torso of the former Špička Gate, from which remains of the Gothic fortifications continue to be visible on the right. After a while he will pass through another baroque gate (Leopold Gate) to the inner Vyšehrad area.

St. Martin rotunda from the 11th century stands right behind the gate. A road passes further beneath it through Vyšehrad all the way to the Masonry Gate, constructed in the 1840's. Then it continues to Podvyšehradí, (meaning area beneath Vyšehrad – a note by the translator) nowadays part of the New Town.

VYŠEHRAD

Grassy area of the Vyšehrad park is proudly guarded by four statuaries, created between 1889–1897 by the famous Czech sculptor J. V. Myslbek, inspired by old Czech legends. They are: Lumír and Song, Ctirad and Šárka, Přemysl and Libuše, and the picture shows Záboj and Slavoj. Long ago, an original Romanesque palace of the Czech princes and then Charles IV used to stand here in these places

This romanesque rotunda of St. Martin is the oldest preserved monument at Vyšehrad. It was built most likely in the second half of the 11th century under the reign of king Vratislav I. Following the establishment of baroque Vyšehrad fortress, it was turned into a gunpowder storage place and then a warehouse. Vyšehrad's capitulum bought it back from the military in the second half of the 19th century and restored it

A vista way goes right from Leopold Gate along the perimeter of the fortification. There are views of the Botič creek valley, remains of the Gothic fortification of New Town, New Town churches founded in Charles's era, and also a view all the way to the Prague Castle. If we set out to the left of the gate, we find views from the height of the bastions to the south at onflowing Vltava and suburbian buildings along its banks. But the most sought-after view is of the entire Prague basin, Castle, and Petřín from the western edge of the fortification. Remains of Gothic fortification with legendary Libuše's bath, originally a watch-house, are situated below on a rock above the river. After a short walk we come to the Vyšehrad park area which Myslbek's statues inspired by Czech legends, whit were originally standing at Palacký Bridge. There used to be the original prince and royal acropolis in the area of the park all the way to the edge of the cliff above the river. There also used to stand palace buildings as well as administration personnel buildings and church structures. Remains of a Romanesque bridge have been preserved to this day. A detailed acquaintance with the Vyšehrad history is provided for visitors at the exposition in the New Deanship or Masonry Gate area, where there is also access to the casemates.

St. Peter and Paul church built in neo-Gothic style deserves to be seen as well. Its construction was completed in 1903 according to the design of Joseph Mocker and František Mikš at the site of the original basilica and then Charles's church. Thus, after a period of Renaissance and baroque restructuring the church returned to its Gothic image, symbolizing ties to Charles's era. The church is well known for its painting of the Virgin Mary of Rain from the period of the second half of the 14th century and a gorgeous folklore painting of the walls, in the Art Nouveau style.

Quite outstanding is the Vyšehrad cemetery, located next to the church. The originaly parish cemetery was recreated in the 19th century thanks to the care of the patriotic abbots of the abbey in the final resting place for personalities of Czech cultural and social life. The cemetery is dominated by Slavín – a common tomb of the most merited sons and daughters of the Czech nation. At the same time, the whole area of the cemetery is a unique gallery of funeral plastic arts, whose authors were outstanding Czech sculptors such as Joseph Václav Myslbek, František Bílek, Bohumil Kafka, Josef Mauder, and others.

Sight-seeing of the romantic Vyšehrad has a number of unusual views of Prague with pleasant strolls through beautiful parks. It attracts visitors new to the city as well as history admirers, lovers, and for its grand peace also many thoughtful people.

MOTHER
OF CITIES

Theme and text by Marie Vitochová and Jindřich Kejř
Photographs by Jiří Všetečka

Cover design and graphic layout by Václav Rytina
Translated into English by Václav Hromas
Published by V Ráji Publishing House as its 52nd publication,
80 pages, 70 color photographs
First edition, 1996
Printed by Východočeská printery, s. r. o., Pardubice